www.booksbyboxer.com

Bee Three Publishing is an imprint of Books By Boxer
Published by
Books By Boxer, Leeds, LS13 4BS, UK
Books by Boxer (EU), Dublin, D02 P593, IRELAND
Boxer Gifts LLC, 955 Sawtooth Oak Cir, VA 22802, USA
© Books By Boxer 2025
cs@boxer.gifts
All Rights Reserved
**MADE IN CHINA**
ISBN: 9781915410870

MIX
Paper
FSC™ C007683

This book is produced from responsibly sourced paper to ensure forest management

# WHAT MAKES A
# GIRL DINNER

GIRL DINNER IS ABOUT EATING WHAT YOU WANT TO EAT, WHETHER IT'S A CHARCUTERIE-ESQUE BOARD WITH OLIVES, CHEESE, BREAD, MEAT, AND NUTS, OR A FEW LOW-EFFORT COMPONENTS PUT TOGETHER.

GIRL DINNER IS THE ULTIMATE LAZY (OR BUSY!) GIRL RECIPE BOOK, WHICH WILL PROVIDE YOU WITH A

# LOW-EFFORT DINNER
# FOR ONE!

# EAT WHAT YOU WANT TO EAT

# WHAT MAKES A
# BALANCED MEAL

WHEN ASSEMBLING YOUR GIRL DINNER,
IT'S IMPORTANT TO BEAR IN MIND WHAT
MAKES A BALANCED MEAL, SO YOU CAN

## ENSURE BOTH YOUR BODY AND SOUL ARE NOURISHED!

THE NEXT FEW PAGES WILL COVER THE
IDEAL PROPORTIONS OF EACH OF THE MAIN
FOOD GROUPS WITHIN YOUR MEALS, AND
EXAMPLES OF WHAT THOSE COULD BE
WITHIN A SNACK PLATE DINNER.

# PROTEIN

## PROTEIN SHOULD MAKE UP AROUND 1/4 OF YOUR PLATE.

PROTEIN IS USED IN OUR BODIES TO MAKE MUSCLES, HAIR, AND SKIN, AMONGST MANY OTHER FUNCTIONS.

# EXAMPLES OF PROTEIN COULD INCLUDE:

- EDAMAME BEANS
- COTTAGE CHEESE
- TINNED FISH
- LENTILS

- DELI MEATS
- CHICKPEAS
- EGGS
- TOFU

# HEALTHY FATS

HEALTHY FATS SHOULD MAKE UP 2 TABLESPOONS OF YOUR PLATE.

HIGH FAT FOODS WTH ADDITIONAL NUTRIENTS MAKE UP AN ESSENTIAL PART OF OUR DIET, BUT THEY ALSO HELP THE MEAL BE EXTRA DELICIOUS!

# EXAMPLES OF HEALTHY FATS INCLUDE:

- NUTS AND SEEDS
- NUT BUTTERS
- FATTY FISH
- CHEESE
- OLIVE OIL
- AVOCADO

# CARBOHYDRATES

CARBOHYDRATES SHOULD MAKE UP 1/4 TO 1/3 OF YOUR PLATE.

CARBOHYDRATES ARE THE MAIN
SOURCE OF ENERGY FOR OUR
CELLS AND BRAINS.

FIBRE-RICH CARBOHYDRATES
HELP WITH SUGAR BALANCE AND
GUT HEALTH.

# EXAMPLES OF CARBOHYDRATES COULD INCLUDE:

- WHOLEGRAIN NAAN OR PITA
- WHOLEGRAIN CRACKERS
- QUINOA
- SWEET POTATOES
- BREAD
- POPCORN
- BROWN RICE

# FRUITS AND VEGETABLES

FRUITS AND VEGETABLES SHOULD MAKE UP 1/2 OF YOUR PLATE.

FRUITS AND VEGGIES PROVIDE YOUR BODY WITH FIBRE, WATER, AND LOTS OF DIFFERENT MICRONUTRIENTS.

MAKE YOUR PLATE AS COLORFUL AS POSSIBLE TO HAVE THE MOST IMPACT!

# EXAMPLES OF FRUIT AND VEG INCLUDE:

- CHERRY TOMATOES
- CUCUMBERS
- BELL PEPPERS
- CARROTS
- BERRIES
- APPLE SLICES
- GRAPES
- MELON

# MEXICAN SNACK PLATE

## WANT TO SPICE UP YOUR GIRL DINNER?

# HERE'S SOME IDEAS FOR A MEXICAN-INSPIRED SNACK PLATE:

- BEANS
- AVOCADO (SLICED OR GUACAMOLE)
- SALSA
- PINEAPPLE
- WATERMELON
- SWEETCORN
- PEPPERS
- SHREDDED CHICKEN
- TORTILLA CHIPS
- CORN TORTILLAS
- CHEDDAR CHEESE
- QUESO FRESCO
- CHORIZO

# ASIAN-INSPIRED SNACK PLATE

## FOR AN ASIAN-INSPIRED GIRL DINNER, YOU MIGHT NEED SOME PRE-MADE ITEMS,

# BUT YOU COULD ALREADY HAVE THEM IN YOUR FRIDGE OR FREEZER:

- PRAWN CRACKERS
- PEANUTS
- SPRING ROLLS
- SEAWEED
- BABY CUCUMBER
- SHREDDED CHICKEN OR BEEF

- GYOZA
- PINEAPPLE
- LYCHEE
- SUGAR SNAP PEAS
- WASABI PEAS
- TOFU
- LETTUCE

# FRENCH SNACK PLATE

## LOOKING FOR A MORE TRADITIONAL CHARCUTERIE BOARD FOR ONE?

# HERE ARE SOME INGREDIENTS YOU COULD INCLUDE IN A FRENCH-INSPIRED GIRL DINNER:

- APPLES
- PROSCIUTTO
- CRACKERS
- ALMONDS
- BABY CARROTS
- STRAWBERRIES

- BRIE
- HAM
- PÂTÉ
- BAGUETTE
- GRAPES
- CORNICHONS

# MEDITERRANEAN SNACK PLATE

## WANT A QUICK, EASY, AND DELICIOUS MEDITERRANEAN-INSPIRED GIRL DINNER?

# HERE'S A FEW IDEAS OF WHAT YOU COULD INCLUDE:

- CHERRY TOMATOES
- APRICOTS
- FIGS
- PITA BREAD
- SLICED CHICKEN
- TINNED FISH
- ROASTED CHICKPEAS

- HUMMUS
- TZATZIKI
- BELL PEPPERS
- FETA CHEESE
- OLIVES
- AVOCADO
- CUCUMBER STICKS

# BREAKFAST FOR GIRL DINNER

## WANT A QUICK, HEALTHY, AND DELICIOUS BREAKFAST?

# WE ALL LOVE BREAKFAST FOR DINNER – AND THIS CHARCUTERIE STYLE BREAKFAST WILL ELEVATE YOUR GIRL DINNER TO THE NEXT LEVEL!

- BANANA
- STRAWBERRIES
- RASPBERRIES
- FIGS
- KIWIS
- BLUEBERRIES
- GRAPES

- YOGHURT
- GRANOLA
- ALMONDS
- HONEY
- JAM
- PEANUT BUTTER
- MINI BAGELS
- WAFFLES

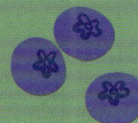

# SPINACH AND SUNDRIED TOMATO FRITATA

HEALTHY AND DELICIOUS, HAVE THESE WONDERFUL FRITATAS AS THE CENTERPIECE OF YOUR SNACK PLATE, OR ON THEIR OWN!

## INGREDIENTS:

- 1 TBSP MINCED GARLIC
- 1 6OZ | 170G BABY SPINACH
- 12 LARGE EGGS, LIGHTLY BEATEN
- 1/2 CUP | 120ML HALF-AND-HALF
- 3/4 CUP | 180ML SHREDDED SHARP CHEDDAR CHEESE
- 3/4 CUP | 180ML DRAINED, CHOPPED SUN-DRIED TOMATOES
- 1/4 TSP | 80G KOSHER SALT
- 1/4 TSP PEPPER

# METHOD:

 **PREP** 10 MINS   **COOK** 12 MINS   **SERVES** 2

**STEP 1**   PREHEAT OVEN TO 375°F / 190°C.

**STEP 2**   ADD GARLIC TO HOT SKILLET AND SAUTÉ 30 SECONDS. ADD SPINACH.

**STEP 3**   COOK 1 MINUTE OR UNTIL WILTED. WHISK TOGETHER EGGS,

**STEP 4**   HALF-AND-HALF, CHEESE, TOMATOES, SALT, PEPPER, IN A LARGE BOWL; GRADUALLY POUR OVER SPINACH MIXTURE IN SKILLET.

**STEP 5**   TRANSFER SKILLET TO OVEN, AND BAKE 20 MINUTES OR UNTIL SET AND BEGINNING TO BROWN.

# CREAMY GARLIC CHICKEN
# QUESADILLA

THIS CREAMY GARLIC QUESADILLA PUTS A TWIST ON THE USUAL MEXICAN CLASSIC – AND YOU'RE GUARANTEED TO LOVE IT.

## INGREDIENTS:

- 1 8OZ | 50G WATERCRESS
- 1/2 SMALL BUNCH OF CHIVES
- 1/2 LEMON, ZESTED
- 5 TBSP GARLIC SOFT CHEESE
- 2 ROASTED CHICKEN BREASTS, SKIN REMOVED AND RESERVED
- 2 LARGE FLOUR TORTILLAS
- 1OZ | 30G MATURE CHEDDAR, GRATED
- 1OZ | 30G MOZZARELLA, GRATED

# METHOD:

 **PREP**
10 MINS

 **COOK**
10 MINS

 **SERVES**
2

**STEP 1** BLITZ THE WATERCRESS, CHIVES, LEMON ZEST, AND SOFT CHEESE TOGETHER, AND SEASON.

**STEP 2** FRY THE RESERVED CHICKEN SKIN FOR 5 MINS UNTIL CRISP, THEN SET ASIDE.

**STEP 3** MEANWHILE, SHRED THE ROASTED CHICKEN. SPREAD THE CHEESE MIX OVER 1 TORTILLA, TOP WITH THE CHICKEN, CRISPY CHICKEN SKIN, THE CHEDDAR, MOZZARELLA, AND SECOND TORTILLA.

**STEP 4** HEAT A FRYING PAN OVER A MEDIUM HEAT, ADD THE QUESADILLA AND COOK FOR 2-3 MINS ON EACH SIDE. CUT INTO FOUR.

# LOADED JACKET POTATO

With crispy skins and a deliciously cheesy and bacon-y inside, these jacket potatoes are well worth the extra effort.

## INGREDIENTS:

- 2 JACKET POTATOES
- 4 RASHERS OF UNSMOKED BACK BACON
- 4.5OZ | 125G MOZZARELLA (SHREDDED)
- 1.5OZ | 40G CHEDDAR (SHREDDED)
- 2 TBSP
- CHIVES (FINELY CHOPPED)

# METHOD:

 **PREP** 10 MINS

 **COOK** 35MINS

**SERVES** 2

**STEP 1** PREHEAT YOUR OVEN TO 200°C / 400°F. STAB TWO POTATOES WITH A FORK, AND MICROWAVE THEM FOR 10 MINUTES, THEN TRANSFER TO THE OVEN FOR 15 MINUTES.

**STEP 2** ADD A DRIZZLE OF VEGETABLE OIL TO A FRYING PAN AND PLACE OVER A MEDIUM-HIGH HEAT UNTIL HOT. FRY THE BACON FOR 2-4 MINUTES ON EACH SIDE UNTIL AT YOUR PREFERRED CRISPINESS.

**STEP 3** SLICE POTATOES IN HALF AND SCOOP OUT THE POTATO FROM THE SKINS, ADDING TO A BOWL.

**STEP 4** CHOP BACON INTO SMALL PIECES AND ADD TO THE BOWL WITH CHIVES AND MOZZARELLA. MIX WELL.

**STEP 5** THEN SPOON BACK ONTO THE POTATO SKINS. SPRINKLE CHEDDAR OVER THE TOP OF EACH POTATO.

**STEP 6** BAKE FOR 4 MINUTES, UNTIL THE CHEESE IS MELTED AND SLIGHTLY BROWN.

# GARLIC BREAD GRILLED CHEESE

A SIMPLE BUT ELEVATED GRILLED CHEESE, IT TAKES NO TIME AT ALL TO MAKE, AND FEELS SO GOOD TO EAT!

## INGREDIENTS:

- 4 SLICES BREAD (ANY KIND)
- 2 TBSP | 30G BUTTER
- 2 GARLIC CLOVES
- 1/2 TSP DRIED OREGANO
- 12OZ | 340G CHEESE (SHREDDED)

(FEEL FREE TO MIX TYPES, CHEDDAR AND MOZZARELLA ARE GOOD!)

# METHOD:

 **PREP** 10 MINS

 **COOK** 10 MINS

 **SERVES** 2

**STEP 1** ADD BUTTER TO A BOWL AND MICROWAVE FOR 30 SECONDS OR UNTIL MELTED. ADD GARLIC AND OREGANO TO THE BOWL.

**STEP 2** GENEROUSLY SPRINKLE CHEESE OVER 2 SLICES OF BREAD, THEN PLACE THE REMAINING BREAD ON TOP.

**STEP 3** BRUSH THE OUTSIDE OF THE BREAD WITH THE BUTTER MIXTURE.

**STEP 4** IN A PAN, COOK THE SANDWICHES BUTTER SIDE DOWN ON A MEDIUM HEAT FOR 4 MINUTES.

**STEP 5** COAT THE OTHER SIDE WITH THE REMAINING BUTTER MIXTURE, THEN FLIP AND COOK FOR ANOTHER 3-4 MINUTES.

# STUFFED PEPPER

WITH VEGETABLES, CARBS, AND HEALTHY FATS, THESE STUFFED PEPPERS WILL FILL YOU UP AND FUEL YOUR BODY.

## INGREDIENTS:

- 2 RED PEPPERS
- 1 POUCH COOKED TOMATO RICE
- 1 TBSP PESTO
- HANDFUL BLACK OLIVES (PITTED)
- 3.5OZ | 100G GOAT'S CHEESE

# METHOD:

 **PREP**
10 MINS

 **COOK**
15 MINS

 **SERVES**
1

**STEP 1** SLICE THE TOP OUT OF 2 PEPPERS AND SCOOP OUT THE SEEDS. COOK IN THE MICROWAVE FOR 5-6 MINS ON HIGH HEAT UNTIL SOFTENED.

**STEP 2** MIX THE RICE POUCH IN A BOWL WITH PESTO, OLIVES, AND 3/4 OF THE GOAT'S CHEESE.

**STEP 3** SCOOP THE MIX INTO BOTH PEPPERS AND TOP WITH THE REMAINING GOAT'S CHEESE, BEFORE COOKING AGAIN FOR 8-10 MINUTES.

# OMELET

OMELETS ARE QUICK AND COMFORTING, AND YOU CAN ADD EXTRA TOPPINGS TO TAKE YOUR GIRL DINNER TO THE NEXT LEVEL!

## INGREDIENTS:

- 1/2 TBSP SALTED BUTTER
- 3 LARGE EGGS
- PINCH SALT AND PEPPER
- 1/4 CUP | 20G SHARP CHEDDAR CHEESE (SHREDDED)

# METHOD:

 **PREP** 10 MINS

 **COOK** 15 MINS

**SERVES** 1

**STEP 1**  IN A BOWL, WHISK THE EGGS UNTIL COMBINED, THEN WHISK IN A PINCH OF SALT AND PEPPER.

**STEP 2**  MELT BUTTER IN A SKILLET ON MEDIUM-LOW HEAT, THEN ADD THE WHISKED EGGS AND TILT THE PAN UNTIL EVENLY SPREAD.

**STEP 3**  ADD THE PAN LID AND COOK OVER MEDIUM-LOW HEAT UNTIL THE EGGS BEGIN TO SET. USE A SPATULA TO PUSH IN THE EGGS SLIGHTLY, THEN TILT THE PAN AGAIN TO DISTRIBUTE ANY UNCOOKED EGGS TO THE EDGES.

**STEP 4**  AFTER 5-6 MINUTES (OR WHEN THE OMELET IS SET), FLIP THE OMELET AND SWITCH OFF THE HEAT.

**STEP 5**  SPRINKLE WITH CHEESE, AND FOLD BEFORE SERVING!

## WHY NOT ADD OTHER TOPPINGS, LIKE BACON, ONIONS, OR ZUCCHINI?

# LOADED NACHOS

A LITTLE EXTRA IS REQUIRED FOR LOADED NACHOS BUT THEY ARE WELL WORTH IT!

## INGREDIENTS:

- 15-20 TORTILLA CHIPS
- 1/2 TBSP OLIVE OIL
- 1/2 CUP | 50G CHOPPED ONIONS
- 1 CLOVE GARLIC (MINCED)
- 5OZ | 140G GROUND BEEF
- 1/8 TSP KOSHER SALT
- 1/8 TSP BLACK PEPPER (COARSELY GROUND)
- 2/3 CUP | 65G CHEDDAR CHEESE (SHREDDED)
- 1 SMALL TOMATO (CHOPPED)
- 1/4 CUP | 45G BLACK OLIVES (SLICED)

# METHOD:

**PREP**
5 MINS

**COOK**
17 MINS

**SERVES**
1

**STEP 1**   PREHEAT YOUR OVEN TO 200°C / 400°F.

**STEP 2**   LINE A TRAY WITH FOIL, THEN SPREAD OUT THE TORTILLA CHIPS EVENLY.

**STEP 3**   HEAT OLIVE OIL IN A SKILLET OVER MEDIUM HEAT, THEN ADD ONIONS AND STIR OCCASIONALLY, COOKING FOR 2 MINUTES. ADD GARLIC, AND COOK FOR 1 MORE MINUTE.

**STEP 4**   ADD GROUND BEEF, SALT, AND PEPPER INTO THE SKILLET AND COOK FOR 8 MINUTES (OR UNTIL BROWNED), STIRRING OCCASIONALLY.

**STEP 5**   TRANSFER THE BEEF TO A PLATE LINED WITH PAPER TOWEL.

**STEP 6**   SPOON BEEF OVER THE TORTILLA CHIPS, THEN ADD CHEESE, TOMATOES, OLIVES, AND ANY OTHER TOPPINGS OF YOUR CHOICE.

**STEP 7**   PLACE THE TRAY INTO THE OVEN, AND BAKE FOR 5 MINUTES OR UNTIL THE CHEESE MELTS.

# 4 QUARTER WRAPS

THESE WENT VIRAL FOR A REASON, QUICK AND EASY TO MAKE BUT OH-SO DELICIOUS!

## INGREDIENTS:

- 1 TORTILLA WRAP
- 4 DIFFERENT FILLINGS WHICH COMPLEMENT EACH OTHER (WE LIKE TOMATO PUREE, CHEESE, TOMATOES, AND PEPPERONI!)

# METHOD:

 **PREP** 10 MINS

 **COOK** 5MINS

 **SERVES** 1

**STEP 1** BEGIN BY SLICING HALFWAY UP A TORTILLA.

**STEP 2** PLACE EACH TOPPING IN A SEPARATE QUARTER OF THE TORTILLA.

**STEP 3** BEGIN FOLDING THE TORTILLA AT EACH QUARTER, STARTING FROM THE BOTTOM WHERE THE SLICE IS.

**STEP 4** ONCE FOLDED COMPLETELY, USE A PAN OR SANDWICH PRESS TO TOAST YOUR WRAP UNTIL TOASTED TO YOUR PREFERENCE!

## MAKE SURE YOUR FILLINGS ARE PRE-COOKED!

# AGLIO E OLIO

Made with only 4 ingredients that we can almost guarantee you have already, you can make a restaurant quality meal in no time at all!

## INGREDIENTS:

- 1/2 cup | 120ml olive oil
- 8 cloves garlic, thinly sliced
- 1/2 tsp crushed red pepper flakes (or more, to taste)
- Salt and pepper to taste

# METHOD:

 **PREP**
2 MINS

 **COOK**
10 MINS

 **SERVES**
2

**STEP 1**   COOK THE SPAGHETTI UNTIL AL DENTE.

**STEP 2**   MEANWHILE, HEAT THE OLIVE OIL IN A LARGE PAN OVER MEDIUM HEAT. ADD THE GARLIC AND PEPPER FLAKES, FRYING FOR 3–5 MINS. DO NOT BURN THE GARLIC.

**STEP 3**   ADD THE SPAGHETTI WHEN READY, THEN TOSS IN THE SAUCE. ADD SEASONING TO TASTE, AND TOP WITH PARSLEY, PARMESAN, AND A SQUEEZE OF LEMON IF YOU HAVE IT (OR WANT TO).

# CROUTONS

Not a meal on their own, but croutons will be the perfect addition to your snack plate dinner

## INGREDIENTS:

- 2 THICK SLICES BREAD
- 2-3 TBSP RAPESEED OIL
- SALT FLAKES

# METHOD:

 **PREP**
5 MINS

 **COOK**
8-10 MINS

 **SERVES**
2

**STEP 1**  PREHEAT THE OVEN TO 160°C / 320°F.

**STEP 2**  SLICE THE BREAD INTO SMALL CUBES.

**STEP 3**  ADD OIL TO A BOWL AND THEN POUR IN
THE BREAD CUBES. TOSS WELL TO COAT,
THEN SPRINKLE WITH SALT.

**STEP 4**  PLACE THE BREAD CUBES EVENLY ONTO
A TRAY, AND BAKE FOR 8-10 MINUTES
(OR UNTIL BROWNED AND CRUNCHY)!

# VEGGIE SKEWERS

Have a load of vegetables you need to use up? Make these delicious veggie skewers! Simple but flavorful.

## INGREDIENTS:

- 2 medium red onion (sliced into 6 chunks)
- 2 medium zucchini – (sliced)
- 1 red bell pepper (de-seeded and sliced)
- 1 orange bell pepper (de-seeded and sliced)
- 1 yellow bell pepper (de-seeded and sliced)
- 1 green bell pepper (de-seeded and sliced)
- Olive oil – for brushing
- Balsamic vinegar – for serving

# METHOD:

**PREP**
15 MINS

**COOK**
8 MINS

**SERVES**
2

**STEP 1**   SOAK 4-6 WOODEN SKEWERS IN WATER FOR AT LEAST 15 MINUTES, TO PREVENT BURNING ON THE GRILL.

**STEP 2**   PREHEAT THE GRILL TO A MEDIUM-HIGH HEAT.

**STEP 3**   SKEWER YOUR VEGGIES BY ALTERNATING EACH TIME, THEN BRUSH EACH SKEWER WITH A DASH OF OLIVE OIL.

**STEP 4**   ADD SKEWERS TO THE GRILL AND COOK FOR 5-8 MINUTES ON EACH SIDE, ONLY REMOVING FROM THE HEAT ONCE THE VEGETABLES ARE ONLY JUST BROWNING AND SOFTENING.

**STEP 5**   DRIZZLE WITH BALSAMIC VINEGAR AND SERVE!

# PEPPERONI PIZZA BAGUETTE

This pepperoni pizza baguette will satiate your cravings, and will become your new favorite easy dinner!

## INGREDIENTS:

- 1 BAGUETTE
- 1/2 CUP | 120ML MARINARA SAUCE
- 1/2 CUP | 50G CHEESE (SHREDDED)
- PEPPERONI SLICES (AS MANY AS YOU WANT)
- FRESH BASIL FOR GARNISH

# METHOD:

**PREP**
5 MINS

**COOK**
10 MINS

**SERVES**
2

**STEP 1**     PREHEAT YOUR OVEN TO 200°C / 400°F.

**STEP 2**     SLICE THE BAGUETTE IN HALF, AND
THEN SLICE IN HALF LENGTHWISE.

**STEP 3**     SPREAD MARINARA SAUCE OVER THE
BAGUETTE SLICES, THEN SPRINKLE ON
CHEESE AND ADD PEPPERONI.

**STEP 4**     PLACE THE BAGUETTES ONTO A BAKING
TRAY AND COOK FOR 7-10 MINUTES
(UNTIL CHEESE IS BUBBLING AND
BAGUETTES ARE WARM).

**WHY NOT EXPERIMENT WITH OTHER
TOPPINGS TO MAKE IT YOUR OWN?**

# BRUSCHETTA

FRESH AND TASTY, BRUSCHETTA IS AN ITALIAN CLASSIC THAT WILL SIT BEAUTIFULLY ALONGSIDE ANY SNACK PLATE DINNER.

## INGREDIENTS:

- 1/2 CUP | 100G TOMATOES (CHOPPED)
- 1 TBSP PARMESAN CHEESE (SHREDDED)
- 1 CLOVE GARLIC (MINCED)
- 1/2 TBSP OLIVE OIL
- 1/4 TSP BALSAMIC VINEGAR
- 1/8 TSP SALT
- 1/8 TSP BLACK PEPPER (FRESHLY GROUND)
- 1 TBSP FRESH BASIL (CHOPPED)
- 4 SLICES BAGUETTE

# METHOD:

 **PREP**
**5 MINS**

 **COOK**
**5 MINS**

 **SERVES**
**2**

**STEP 1**  PREHEAT YOUR OVEN TO 230°C / 450°F.

**STEP 2**  PLACE TOMATO INTO A BOWL, THEN STIR
IN THE PARMESAN, OLIVE OIL, GARLIC,
BALSAMIC VINEGAR, SALT, AND PEPPER.
ADD BASIL TO THE MIXTURE AND STIR
AGAIN.

**STEP 3**  GENTLY BRUSH ONE SIDE OF THE BREAD
SLICES WITH OLIVE OIL, THEN PLACE
THEM ONTO A TRAY WITH ALUMINUM
FOIL.

**STEP 4**  TOAST IN THE OVEN FOR 5–6 MINUTES (OR
UNTIL LIGHTLY BROWNED ON THE EDGES).

**STEP 5**  PLACE THE BREAD ON A PLATE (OLIVE OIL
SIDE UP), THEN TOP WITH THE TOMATO
MIXTURE.

# PESTO PASTA

THE WORLD-FAVORITE PESTO PASTA. AS SIMPLE AS SIMPLE CAN BE. IT PROVES YOU CAN GET BIG FLAVOR WITH LITTLE EFFORT!

## INGREDIENTS:

- 2OZ | 60G SPAGHETTI (OR ANY PASTA YOU HAVE TO HAND)
- 1/2 TBSP PESTO
- 1-2 TBSP PASTA WATER
- 2 TBSP PARMESAN CHEESE (SHREDDED)

# METHOD:

 **PREP** 5 MINS

 **COOK** 10 MINS

 **SERVES** 1

**STEP 1** BRING A PAN OF WATER TO BOIL, THEN ADD YOUR SPAGHETTI AND COOK AS THE INSTRUCTIONS ON THE PACKAGING.

**STEP 2** RESERVE 1/4 CUP OF PASTA WATER BEFORE DRAINING.

**STEP 3** PLACE PASTA INTO A BOWL AND MIX PESTO AND 1-2 TABLESPOONS OF THE PASTA WATER (UNTIL SOFT IN TEXTURE).

**STEP 4** SPRINKLE PARMESAN OVER THE PASTA, AND SERVE!

# AVOCADO TOAST

WITH DELICIOUS HEALTHY FATS FROM THE AVOCADO, PAIRED WITH SOME SIDES. THE CLASSIC AVOCADO TOAST MAKES A GREAT GIRL DINNER!

## INGREDIENTS:

- 1 SLICE OF BREAD
- 1/2 RIPE AVOCADO
- 1/8 TSP KOSHER SALT
- 1/8 TSP BLACK PEPPER (COARSELY GROUND)
- 1/2 TSP EXTRA VIRGIN OLIVE OIL
- 1 TOMATO (SLICED)

# METHOD:

 **PREP 5 MINS**

 **COOK 5 MINS**

 **SERVES 1**

**STEP 1**   TOAST THE SLICE OF BREAD UNTIL GOLDEN BROWN IN COLOR.

**STEP 2**   SCOOP AVOCADO OUT OF THE SKIN AND MASH IN A SMALL BOWL WITH A FORK, THEN SEASON WITH SALT AND PEPPER.

**STEP 3**   SPREAD AVOCADO GENEROUSLY ON THE TOAST, TOP WITH TOMATO, AND DRIZZLE WITH OLIVE OIL.

# MINI QUICHES

Easy crustless quiches that take hardly any time to make – means more time preparing the rest of your snack plate!

## INGREDIENTS:

- 3 eggs
- 1 1/2 tbsp milk
- 1/4 tsp mixed herbs
- 1/8 tsp salt
- 1/8 tsp pepper
- 1/4 cup | 30g chicken, bacon (diced and cooked), or vegetables (finely diced)
- 1/2 cup | 50g cheese (grated)

# METHOD:

**PREP**
**5 MINS**

**COOK**
**15 MINS**

**SERVES**
**1**

**STEP 1** PREHEAT OVEN TO 180°C / 355°F. SPRAY A MUFFIN TRAY WITH COOKING OIL.

**STEP 2** ADD THE EGGS AND MILK TO A MEDIUM BOWL AND WHISK WELL.

**STEP 3** ADD THE HERBS AND SEASONING, WHISK WELL, THEN ADD THE CHEESE, AND MEAT OR VEGETABLES.

**STEP 4** SPOON THE MIXTURE INTO THE MUFFIN TRAY, THEN BAKE FOR 15-18 MINUTES.

**STEP 5** ALLOW TO COOL IN THE MUFFIN TRAY, THEN ENJOY.

# PRAWN AND COCONUT SOUP

WARMING AND FLAVORSOME, THIS SOUP IS SUPER QUICK TO MAKE BUT TASTES RESTAURANT QUALITY!

## INGREDIENTS:

- 3 TBSP THAI GREEN CURRY PASTE
- 14OZ | 400ML CAN COCONUT MILK
- 5OZ | 150G COOKED PRAWNS
- 9OZ | 250G PACK COURGETTI

# METHOD:

**PREP**
0 MINS

**COOK**
5 MINS

**SERVES**
2

**STEP 1**    HEAT OIL IN A FRYING PAN, THEN ADD THE CURRY PASTE AND COOK FOR 1 MIN.

**STEP 2**    ADD THE COCONUT MILK, LET BUBBLE FOR A FEW MINUTES, THEN ADD THE REMAINING INGREDIENTS.

**STEP 3**    SEASON AS NECESSARY, WHEN WARMED THROUGH SERVE AND ENJOY!

# CROISSANT SANDWICH

Have you got some croissants left over from breakfast? Make them into a super easy and delicious savory dinner.

## INGREDIENTS:

### HAM AND CHEESE

- HAM AND CHEESE
- GOUDA CHEESE
- PROSCIUTTO
- HONEY MUSTARD
- OLIVE OIL

### CAPRESE

- BASIL PESTO
- MOZZARELLA
- CHERRY TOMATOES
- SUNDRIED TOMATOES
- ARUGULA

# METHOD:

**PREP**
**2 MINS**

**COOK**
**5 MINS**

**SERVES**
**1**

**STEP 1**   BAKE YOUR FILLED CROISSANTS IN THE OVEN UNTIL CRISPY AND THE CHEESE IS MELTED, AROUND 5 MINS.

**STEP 2**   WE RECOMMEND SERVING YOUR CROISSANT SANDWICH WITH SOME EXTRA PICKY-BITS ON THE SIDE!

# VEGGIE STIR-FRY

A SUPER EASY DINNER FOR WHEN YOU HAVE SOME VEG THAT NEEDS USING UP AND SOME NOODLES IN THE CUPBOARD.

## INGREDIENTS:

SOME SUGGESTIONS ARE:
- RED PEPPER
- CARROT
- COURGETTE
- SUGAR SNAP PEAS

OTHER INGREDIENTS:
- AN INCH OF GINGER
- 1 GARLIC CLOVE
- 2 TBSP SOY SAUCE
- 2 TBSP HOISIN SAUCE
- 1 GREEN ONION

# METHOD:

 **PREP**
5 MINS

 **COOK**
10 MINS

 **SERVES**
1

**STEP 1**   FRY THE GREEN ONIONS, GARLIC, AND GINGER TOGETHER IN A WOK, THEN ADD ALL OF YOUR VEGETABLES, FRY FOR A FEW MORE MINUTES, KEEPING EVERYTHING MOVING AROUND.

**STEP 2**   ADD YOUR SAUCES AND A SPLASH OF WATER, COOKING FOR ANOTHER FEW MINUTES UNTIL THE VEGETABLES ARE COOKED.

**STEP 3**   ADD COOKED NOODLES, TOSS WELL, THEN ENJOY.

# ENGLISH MUFFIN PIZZAS

THESE ENGLISH MUFFIN PIZZAS ARE EASY TO MAKE AND YOU CAN DRESS THEM UP HOW YOU WANT!

## INGREDIENTS:

- 2 ENGLISH MUFFINS
- CANNED PIZZA SAUCE
- SHREDDED CHEESE
- YOUR DESIRED TOPPINGS

# METHOD:

 **PREP**
3 MINS

 **COOK**
10 MINS

 **SERVES**
1

**STEP 1** CUT THE ENGLISH MUFFINS IN HALF, THEN PLACE CUT-SIDE UP ON A BAKING SHEET.

**STEP 2** COVER THE TOPS WITH PIZZA SAUCE.

**STEP 3** ADD THE SHREDDED CHEESE TO YOUR LIKING.

**STEP 4** ADD ANY FURTHER TOPPINGS FROM YOUR FRIDGE (WHAT ABOUT PEPPERONI, OLIVES, SWEETCORN, SPINACH, OR MUSHROOMS?)

**STEP 5** BAKE IN THE OVEN FOR 10 MINS AT 190°C / 375°F.

# 'FANCY' RAMEN

DO YOU HAVE SOME INSTANT RAMEN IN YOUR CUPBOARD BUT DON'T FEEL LIKE IT'S ENOUGH? ADD ANYTHING TO IT TO ELEVATE IT INTO A FANCY GIRL DINNER!

## INGREDIENTS:

- 1 RAMEN PACKET
- TOPPINGS OF YOUR CHOICE

THESE COULD BE:
- BROCCOLI
- TOFU / CHICKEN
- CARROT
- EGG
- SUGAR SNAP PEAS
- SEAWEED
- SESAME SEEDS
- GREEN ONION

# METHOD:

 **PREP**
5 MINS

 **COOK**
10 MINS

 **SERVES**
1

**STEP 1**  ADD SOME WATER TO A PAN, THEN ADD THE RAMEN SEASONINGS.

**STEP 2**  ADD YOUR DESIRED VEG AND PROTEIN, THEN COOK FOR A FEW MINUTES.

**STEP 3**  ADD THE INSTANT NOODLES AND COOK BY THE PACKAGE INSTRUCTIONS.

**STEP 4**  ADD ANY EXTRA TOPPINGS AND SOME SOY SAUCE TO TASTE.

# SHREDDED CHICKEN TACOS

IDEAL FOR WHEN YOU HAVE LEFTOVER CHICKEN BUT AREN'T SURE WHAT TO DO WITH IT! NO TORTILLAS? PUT THE CHICKEN ON THE NACHOS!

## INGREDIENTS:

- 3 CUPS | 375G SHREDDED ROTISSERIE CHICKEN
- 1 TBSP CHILI POWDER
- 1 TSP CUMIN
- 1 TSP GARLIC POWDER
- 1/2 TSP ONION POWDER
- 1/2 TSP SMOKED PAPRIKA
- 1/2 TSP DRIED OREGANO
- 1/2 TSP SALT
- 1/4 CAYENNE PEPPER
- 1 CAN CHOPPED TOMATOES
- 1/4 CUP | 60ML WATER
- 1 CHOPPED GREEN CHILI
- 2 TBSP TOMATO PASTE
- CORN TORTILLAS

# METHOD:

 **PREP 3 MINS**

 **COOK 10 MINS**

 **SERVES 2**

**STEP 1** HEAT YOUR CHICKEN AND SPICES IN A LARGE PAN, COATING EVENLY. ADD IN ALL THE REST OF THE INGREDIENTS (BAR THE TORTILLAS), COOKING UNTIL HEATED.

**STEP 2** LOAD ONTO TORTILLAS WITH YOUR FAVORITE TOPPINGS YOU HAVE ON HAND (CHEESE, JALAPEÑOS, LETTUCE, GUACAMOLE, SALSA?)

WE RECOMMEND MAKING A LARGE PORTION OF THE SPICE MIX TO HAVE ON HAND FOR ANY OF YOUR MEXICAN COOKING NEEDS!

# MEDITERRANEAN COUSCOUS SALAD

REQUIRING VIRTUALLY NO EFFORT EXCEPT FOR CHOPPING UP SOME VEGGIES, THIS COUSCOUS SALAD IS NUTRITIOUS AND TRULY DELICIOUS.

## INGREDIENTS:

- 1 1/2 CUPS | 170G DRIED COUSCOUS
- 1 1/2 CUPS | 355ML BOILING WATER
- DICED VEGGIES OF YOUR CHOICE
- SALT
- JUICE OF HALF A LEMON
- 1 TBSP OLIVE OIL
- CHOPPED PARSLEY

### WE RECOMMEND:

- 1 CUP | 175G DICED BELL PEPPER
- 1/4 CUP | 25G DICED RED ONION
- 1/4 CUP | 45G SLICED BLACK OLIVES
- 1 TBSP CAPERS

# METHOD:

**PREP
5 MINS**

**COOK
5 MINS**

**SERVES
2**

**STEP 1**   IN A LARGE BOWL, ADD THE COUSCOUS, SALT, AND BOILING WATER. MIX, THEN ADD A LID (OR PLATE) TO COVER FOR 5 MINS.

**STEP 2**   FLUFF WITH A FORK, THEN ADD THE VEGETABLES, STIR AND ENJOY.

WANT SOME ADDED PROTEIN? ADD IN SOME CHICKEN, TOFU, OR CHICKPEAS!

# TORTELLINI SOUP

LOW EFFORT BUT DELICIOUS AND FILLING,
MAKE A FANCY-LOOKING SOUP FROM BASIC
INGREDIENTS AND SOME TORTELLINI!

## INGREDIENTS:

- 1 PACK OF TORTELLINI
- 1 CAN OF TOMATOES
- 3 CUPS | 700ML OF
  VEGETABLE STOCK
- A FEW LARGE
  HANDFULS OF SPINACH

# METHOD:

 **PREP**
2 MINS

 **COOK**
5 MINS

 **SERVES**
2

**STEP 1** ADD YOUR STOCK AND CHOPPED TOMATOES TO A SAUCEPAN.

**STEP 2** ADD THE SPINACH AND THE TORTELLINI. BUBBLE UNTIL THE TORTELLINI IS HOT. SEASON WITH SALT AND PEPPER. ADD SOME DRIED ITALIAN HERBS IF DESIRED. THEN TOP WITH PARMESAN.

ADD ANY EXTRA VEG OR PROTEIN YOU HAVE ON HAND TO ELEVATE THIS SOUP EVEN FURTHER!

# QUESADILLAS

Simple and delicious, the Mexican quesadilla will become your go-to when you have leftover tortillas!

## INGREDIENTS:

- 2 corn tortillas
- 1/4 cup | 30g shredded mozzarella
- toppings of choice

These could be:
- black olives
- avocado
- salsa
- sweetcorn
- beans
- jalapeños

# METHOD:

**PREP**
1 MINS

**COOK**
5 MINS

**SERVES**
1

**STEP 1** HEAT A LARGE FRYING PAN THEN PLACE A TORTILLA ON IT. LET COOK FOR A MIN, THEN FLIP. WHEN FLIPPED, ADD 1/2 OF THE CHEESE, FOLLOWED BY WHICHEVER TOPPINGS YOU HAVE.

**STEP 2** PLACE ANOTHER TORTILLA ON TOP, THEN PUT THE LID ON THE PAN. AFTER A MINUTE, FLIP THE QUESADILLA. ONCE THE CHEESE IS MELTED, SERVE.

# HALLOUMI WRAP

MAKE A QUICK WRAP WITH DELICIOUS INGREDIENTS YOU LIKELY ALREADY HAVE IN YOUR FRIDGE.

## INGREDIENTS:

- 3 1/2 OZ | 100G HALLOUMI
- 1 TBSP OLIVE OIL
- 1 LARGE TORTILLA WRAP
- 3 TBSP HUMMUS
- 1 CARROT, PEELED INTO RIBBONS
- HANDFUL OF SPINACH

# METHOD:

 **PREP** 2 MINS  **COOK** 5 MINS  **SERVES** 1

**STEP 1**   SLICE THE HALLOUMI INTO THICK STRIPS AND SEASON WITH PEPPER.

**STEP 2**   FRY THE HALLOUMI FOR A FEW MINUTES ON A LOW-MEDIUM HEAT, ON BOTH SIDES UNTIL GOLDEN.

**STEP 3**   WARM THE TORTILLA (ON A PAN OR IN AN OVEN FOR A FEW MINS), THEN COVER THE INSIDE WITH HUMMUS, ADD THE CARROT, SPINACH, AND HALLOUMI. TOP WITH YOUR FAVORITE SAUCE.

**STEP 4**   ADD ANY OTHER TOPPINGS YOU DESIRE – OLIVES, RED ONION, RED CABBAGE!

**DON'T HAVE HALLOUMI? SWAP IN CHICKEN, TOFU, OR ANY OTHER PROTEIN YOU HAVE ON HAND!**

# SWEET TREATS

## NO GIRL DINNER IS COMPLETE WITHOUT A SWEET TREAT.

MAYBE YOU'RE HAPPY
WITH A FEW CHUNKS OF
DARK CHOCOLATE, BUT IF
YOU WANT SOMETHING A
LITTLE MORE

INDULGENT,

THEN THESE DELICIOUS
DESSERTS MIGHT BE
JUST THE THING!

# NUTELLA & STRAWBERRIES

FOR A LITTLE SWEET TREAT ON THE SIDE OF YOUR SNACK PLATE, HOW ABOUT SOME NUTELLA AND STRAWBERRIES?

## INGREDIENTS:

- GRAHAM CRACKERS
- NUTELLA
- STRAWBERRIES (HALVED)

# METHOD:

 **PREP**
1 MINS

 **COOK**
2 MINS

 **SERVES**
1

**STEP 1**    SPREAD NUTELLA OVER THE GRAHAM CRACKERS. THEN PLACE A STRAWBERRY HALF ON TOP.

**STEP 2**    PLACE A FEW OF THESE DELICIOUS BITES ON THE SIDE OF YOUR SNACK PLATE FOR A SWEET TREAT AND A PORTION OF FRUIT!

CHOCO

# YOGURT BARK

PUT THIS YOGURT BARK ON THE SIDE OF YOUR SNACK PLATE, TOP YOUR GRANOLA OR CEREAL WITH IT – OR JUST HAVE IT AS A SNACK!

## INGREDIENTS:

- 2 CUPS | 475ML FULL FAT VANILLA YOGURT
- 1/2 CUP | 85G STRAWBERRIES
- 1/4 CUP | 85G BLUEBERRIES
- 1/4 CUP | 30G GRANOLA

# METHOD:

 **PREP**
2 MINS

 **COOK**
3 HRS

 **SERVES**
6

**STEP 1** LINE A BAKING SHEET WITH PARCHMENT PAPER.

**STEP 2** SPREAD THE YOGURT EVENLY OVER THE SHEET.

**STEP 3** TOP WITH THE FRUIT AND GRANOLA.

**STEP 4** LEAVE IN THE FREEZER FOR 2–3 HOURS, UNTIL FIRM.

**STEP 5** CUT (OR SMASH) INTO PIECES, AND ENJOY!

# MUG CAKE

A SINGLE-SERVING CAKE COOKED IN A MUG IN THE MICROWAVE – SIGN ME UP!

## INGREDIENTS:

- 1/4 CUP | 30G ALL-PURPOSE FLOUR
- 2 TBSP COCOA POWDER
- 1/4 TSP BAKING POWDER
- 2 TBSP GRANULATED SUGAR
- 1/8 TSP KOSHER SALT
- 1/4 CUP | 60ML MILK
- 2 TBSP VEGETABLE OIL
- 1 TBSP CHOCOLATE SPREAD (OR CHOC CHIPS)

# METHOD:

**PREP**
2 MINS

**COOK**
2 MINS

**SERVES**
1

**STEP 1** ADD THE DRY INGREDIENTS TO A LARGE MUG, THEN WHISK TOGETHER GENTLY.

**STEP 2** ADD THE MILK AND VEGETABLE OIL, AND WHISK GENTLY UNTIL THERE ARE NO CLUMPS.

**STEP 3** ADD YOUR CHOSEN TOPPING ON TOP OF THE BATTER.

**STEP 4** PLACE YOUR MUG ON TOP OF A PAPER TOWEL IN THE MICROWAVE, AND MICROWAVE FOR 70–90 SECONDS.

IF YOURS IS NOT FULLY DONE, MICROWAVE FOR LONGER AT 10 SECOND INTERVALS. BE CAREFUL REMOVING FROM THE MICROWAVE – IT WILL BE HOT!

# SKILLET COOKIE

MAKE YOURSELF A DELICIOUS GOOEY, WARM COOKIE BAKED IN A SMALL SKILLET. THE PERFECT EASY-TO-MAKE DESSERT.

## INGREDIENTS:

- 6 TBSP MELTED BUTTER
- 1/4 CUP | 50G GRANULATED SUGAR
- 1/2 CUP | 90G BROWN SUGAR, TIGHTLY PACKED
- 1 EGG
- 1 TSP VANILLA EXTRACT
- 1 CUP | 120G FLOUR
- 1/2 TSP BAKING POWDER
- PINCH SEA SALT
- 1/2 CUP | 100G CHOCOLATE CHIPS

# METHOD:

 PREP 5 MINS

 COOK 15 MINS

 SERVES 1

**STEP 1** PREHEAT THE OVEN TO 175°C / 350°F. THEN GREASE A 6-INCH NON-STICK SKILLET.

**STEP 2** MIX MELTED BUTTER, GRANULATED SUGAR, AND BROWN SUGAR IN A MIXING BOWL.

**STEP 3** ADD EGG AND VANILLA EXTRACT INTO THE BOWL AND MIX TO COMBINE.

**STEP 4** FOLD IN THE CHOCOLATE CHIPS THEN SPREAD INTO THE SKILLET, ADDING MORE CHOCOLATE CHIPS OR A SPRINKLE OF SEA SALT.

**STEP 5** BAKE FOR 15-20 MINUTES (OR UNTIL YOUR PREFERRED DONENESS).

**STEP 6** REMOVE FROM THE OVEN AND ENJOY!

# CINNAMON SUGAR TORTILLA CHIPS

**THESE CRISPY, SWEET CHIPS ARE THE PERFECT SWEET TREAT FOR WHEN YOU ALSO HAVE SOME TORTILLAS THAT NEED USING UP.**

## INGREDIENTS:

- 3 TORTILLAS
- 2 TBSP. BUTTER
- 1/2 TSP CINNAMON
- 2 TBSP SUGAR

# METHOD:

 **PREP**
1 MINS

 **COOK**
5 MINS

 **SERVES**
2

**STEP 1** PREHEAT THE OVEN TO 175°C / 350°F. THEN SPREAD BUTTER ALL OVER THE TORTILLAS.

**STEP 2** MIX THE SUGAR AND CINNAMON TOGETHER. THEN SPRINKLE THE MIX OVER THE TORTILLAS.

**STEP 3** BAKE FOR 5 TO 8 MINUTES, THEN ENJOY!

# FRUIT SALAD

THIS MIX OF FRUIT WILL BE DELICIOUS ON THE SIDE OF YOUR SNACK PLATE! JUST USE WHAT YOU HAVE AT HAND!

## INGREDIENTS:

- 2 KIWI
- 1 MANGO
- 5.5OZ | 150G PINEAPPLE
- 3.5OZ | 100G GRAPES
- 14OZ | 400G MIXED BERRIES
- 1 LARGE ORANGE
- 2 TSP HONEY

# METHOD:

 **PREP** 10 MINS

 **COOK** 30 MINS

 **SERVES** 4

**STEP 1**  USE A SERRATED KNIFE TO PREPARE THE FRUITS, CUTTING EACH FRUIT INTO SMALL SLICES, REMOVING THE MEMBRANES WHERE APPLICABLE. PUT THE FRUIT IN THE BOWL.

**STEP 2**  SQUEEZE THE SKIN OF THE ORANGE OVER THE BOWL, THEN ADD HONEY AND GENTLY MIX. LEAVE IN THE FRIDGE FOR 30 MINUTES FOR THE JUICES TO BLEND.

# BREAD PUDDING

THIS COMFORTING DESSERT IS MADE WITH LEFTOVER BREAD AND OTHER INGREDIENTS YOU PROBABLY HAVE AT HOME.

## INGREDIENTS:

- 1 EGG
- 2 TBSP MILK
- 2 TBSP CREAM
- 1 TSP VANILLA
- 2 TBSP SUGAR
- PINCH OF SALT
- 1 CUP STALE BREAD
  (2 SLICES, CUT UP)

# METHOD:

**PREP** 15 MINS · **COOK** 10 MINS · **SERVES** 1

**STEP 1**   PREHEAT THE OVEN TO 180°C / 355°F. PUT THE CUT UP PIECES OF BREAD IN THE SINGLE SERVING RAMEKIN.

**STEP 2**   IN A MIXING BOWL, WHISK THE EGGS, SUGAR, VANILLA, CREAM, AND MILK TOGETHER UNTIL SMOOTH.

**STEP 3**   POUR YOUR CUSTARD MIXTURE OVER THE BREAD RAMEKIN, LETTING IT SOAK FOR 5-10 MINS. THEN BAKE IN THE OVEN FOR 8-10 MINS UNTIL GOLDEN AND CRUSTY.

**STEP 4**   ENJOY WARM!

# TOPPED ICE CREAM

ALMOST EVERYONE'S FAVORITE DESSERT – ICE CREAM! WE SUGGEST ELEVATING YOUR ICE CREAM BY ADDING SOME OF THESE TOPPINGS!

## INGREDIENTS:

- CHOPPED NUTS
- FRUITS (BANANA, MIXED BERRIES, LEMON ZEST)
- GRANOLA
- COOKIES (CRUMBLE ON TOP FOR EXTRA DELICIOUSNESS!)
- BROWNIES
- CARAMEL OR FRUIT SAUCE
- NUT BUTTER
- CAKE
- NUTELLA
- CINNAMON
- GRAHAM CRACKER CRUMBS
- HONEY

# METHOD:

 **PREP**
2 MINS

 **COOK**
0 MINS

 **SERVES**
1

**STEP 1** PILE YOUR ICE CREAM INTO THE BOWL
AND SCATTER OVER YOUR TOPPINGS OF
CHOICE. TOP WITH A SAUCE

**STEP 2** ENJOY!

# RICE KRISPIE MUG TREAT

Sticky and delicious, 3 ingredients and ready in under 5 minutes, this will perfect your girl dinner!

## INGREDIENTS:

- 1/2 TBSP BUTTER (UNSALTED)
- 1 CUP | 30G RICE KRISPIES
- 1 1/4 CUP | 75G MINI MARSHMALLOWS (OR 9 SINGLE LARGE)

# METHOD:

**PREP**
0 MINS

**COOK**
3 MINS

**SERVES**
1

**STEP 1**   IN A MICROWAVEABLE MUG, HEAT THE BUTTER AND MARSHMALLOWS IN 30 SECOND BURSTS UNTIL MELTED.

**STEP 2**   MIX THE MIXTURE, THEN STIR IN THE RICE KRISPIES QUICKLY, UNTIL WELL COMBINED.

**STEP 3**   ENJOY!